Nigel Jarrett is a freelance writer and a winner of the Rhys Davies Award for short fiction. His début collection of stories, *Funderland*, was published by Parthian in 2011 to widespread acclaim and long-listed for the Edge Hill Prize. He is a former daily-newspaper journalist. Since 1987 he has been music critic of the *South Wales Argus* and he reviews jazz for *Jazz Journal* and poetry for *Acumen*. He lives in Monmouthshire with his wife, Ann, a former teacher.

Miners at the Quarry Pool

Nigel Jarrett

PARTHIAN

Parthian
The Old Surgery
Napier Street
Cardigan
SA43 1ED

www.parthianbooks.com

First published in 2013

ISBN 9781909844063

Editor: Alan Kellermann
Cover featuring a pastel drawing by Nigel Jarrett
Typeset by Elaine Sharples
Printed and bound by lightningsource.com

Published with the financial support of the Welsh Books Council.

British Library Cataloguing in Publication Data

A cataloguing record for this book is available from the British Library.

‘Obviously it is more exciting to express fifty sensations with one mark than the other way round. One wants the richest possible materials and richest possible sensibility of subject expressed in the most economical way.’

Frank Auerbach, quoted in *The School of London: The Resurgence of Contemporary Painting*, by Alistair Hicks (Phaidon 1989)

This collection is dedicated to the memory of my coalminer grandfathers, who, as far as I could tell, never saw themselves as iconic sons of toil. One was an easygoing chapel organist, the other saturnine and for a while depressive. Both were subsistence gardeners in the General Strike. They burrowed daily into the flanks of Mynydd Maen, never certain that they would emerge unscathed or even alive. Self-educated, they would have known that there was more to the eponymous miners and quarry pool than first appeared and that death's dominion was pretty much irresistible. Being Non-Conformist and subterranean, they saw the light but it was at the end of a tunnel. I'd guess that some of these things have been handed down.

Contents

A Shepherd Learns to Read

A Gulliver among quizzical pullets
was how they found him;
beamed in a barn with no curtain,
a bucolic tragedy.

Now, he's up, a new heart
urging him to an old endeavour
ditched for survival's sake
(dust echo of books banged shut).

He is tortured by diphthongs,
ankle-tapped by silent Ms;
his jaw drops to net
Phthisis, Nuance, Ukulele.

His hands are calloused hills;
blistered escarpments
slope to thin rivers of grit
and dirt horizons, beyond finger-spits.

But, planted each side
of the pages' valley, they
merge to Loxridge Tump
and stout Bwlch-bran.

Between them he will
whistle-in words till
they wheel to a white knot,
an omphalos.

The Jewish Cemetery at Eberswalde

This place does not exist. There are no departed here,
no dead; nor does the yew send shoots
in search of rifts among the Waldens.
Karnilova the draper occupies no plot
in the suit he hid from Fruma-Sarah till his dying day;
Chava and Pilz brook no deep melting
of their feud at Angermunde;
Rosenfeld clutches no posy, Kalisch no twirl of hair;
no snap of tiny Abraham smiles on the chest
of Moshkovitch, like a pressed immortal.
This is unturned soil.
Here no withering volume of Talmudic law
troubles Greta Libin's corpse.

Picking up the Grandchildren

It's his first time at the nursery,
so he practises the password
memorised to prove he's no perv:
Dukey, their cat's name.

Before that he wades
among the white rabbits,
their eyes little eruptions of flesh.
He imagines the worst –

a pile-up of police cars,
and clumps of worried parents,
the echoes of pithead women
queuing to become widows.

But 'Dukey' animates smiles,
gaining him access to the innocents
and their druidic ceremonies
in lollipop-forest clearings.

Tommy peels from a ruck
at his initiate's approach, dabs him
crimson and ochre, whispers
some garbled brotherhood gossip.

Polly is asleep on the annexe bean-bag,
but first he must scuff the gravel outside
for her brother's dinosaur bone, and he sees it,
a long line of hills, rough as pumice.

The joker's graveyard is opposite.
Its diggers hold in aching backs.
He's a chauffeur to royalty, all eyes.
No demon shall prevail.

Ars Longa, Vita Brevis

The widow of poet Tom Lynch's angling buddy
asked him to sow her husband's ashes
on the sliding Pere Maquette they'd fished,
catapulting bait upstream so that it returned
to them as they cast among the innocents.
The idea, you see, was that he would be
fed to the frisky trout as atonement
for all those dawns of riparian pleasure.
Lynch called it *cremorialisation*, but never
cast backwards for examples from history.
So here's my favourite, with apologies
to the other occupation he never sullied with levity:
to be well ground with Veronese's burnt umber
and circulated unseen at the Cana marriage.

Sitting with Aunty Vi

It was a whispered brief, gin on the breath:
Come by whenever you like and say what you've seen.
Conspiratorial closeness, smooth distrust of other informants.

Naturally, I thought she meant a round-up
of the week's events in the village – half an hour
at most, I reckoned, over a Camp coffee,

though there would be other strong stuff:
the stable boy – a burden now – kicked by a mare,
And Mrs Jephcott, thrice naked at an upstairs window.

(That's apart from the resident sparrow-hawk,
crashing in now-you-see-me mode against the laurel and
erupting feather-trailed with a clutch of redstarts).

Blind since birth, she'd had her time, before
the Somme sucked in her man and the queue was spurned.
She fingered his gong's merry-go-round Braille

and read his other belongings in a scalloped tin:
a comma of her hair, one Charles-Hubert watch,
the German's lighter he filched, still reeking.

With whiskered smile and eyes flickering beyond me
at some sisterly accomplice, she said she'd been
singled out, but 'too late to fall beneath a king's horse',

though I could see her being led to a railing
with hectoring comrades hatched from a Tissot,
hear the rustle of *mantelets* and *redingotes*.

So I described autumn's starling clouds ('a million minions
leaderless'); the immigrant's joy and pain;
silent arrowhead jets; Huppert in *The Piano Teacher*.

Courting, I thought she craved more – her eyes on fire
like a dreamer's and her spinster's unseeing told me so:
our heartbeats; our mimicry of sleep, then sleep itself.

For you know that once, prim and attentive,
you inched your knees apart as I took your hand
and she seemed to sigh at a blurred quickening of desire.

Friend in Need

He was so down that day
I couldn't help giving advice.
I'm no agony aunt
and to tell the truth
he accepted it knowing
that I'm hardly qualified,
doing battle with him outdoors
(familiar theatres, redoubts
as wobbly as before and littered
with discarded plans of defence).

I'll talk to her, he said,
but I knew he wouldn't,
the ironing in neat piles and all,
his balled socks in the drawer
a tray of faggots.

Death Studies

Lowell was around here all the time,
a fusspot borrowing sugar and shears
but with a nice line in unburdening,
the hours marked by empty Budweisers
and squashed teabags blocking the sink,
not to mention his fag-ends and fug.

There was the son giving him grief;
the petulant daughter in Finland
(though she had spoilt kids of her own);
and the women – old flames flickering
as he played the awkward fireman;
and the new one, out for the time being.

To be told to then was better than telling,
that sigh when you asked if all was OK
and settled down for the cracking story about
the time Mrs Lowell number two, *petite*,
felled his drunken redwood frame
and, screeching, held a knife to his throat.

Then you realised these were contagions:
instead of worrying about old Mr Hinksman,
who says his wife out there is a cold-caller,
or about the oil-slick motion of the dispossessed,
you sit on your own with a drink at dusk,
picking at ancient signatures of self-harm.

So I often take to hiding when Lowell knocks.
I can hear him outside, calling my name,
walking the perimeter in those muddy brogues,
but I am thinking of the grateful Hinksmans and seeking
words for what awaits them:
landfall's opposite, maybe, then swaying depths.

Ecce Homo

When I go back panda-faced again,
she tut-tuts while he just sits there
watching *Strictly* and wondering why
I don't duck and dive more
like he used to, Forces middleweight.

Or *Get the hell out, girl!* – as if
I'm still his golden Gingham kid
with dimples and cold knees, clutching
that greaseproof pack at the mill door
while his aproned pals gawk like Masons.

There was no name for it then –
steelman stinking of oily filings
who'd 'gone forward' for Billy Graham,
now dumping himself, a billet, on the bed,
and 'healing' with palms under the sheet.

Just a few times – a rash – then nothing.
I swear she'd cottoned on somehow.
I'll swing for you, he'd say, Mr Foxtrot.
God, I sometimes wish he had –
and his effing son-in-law with him.

Nocturne

The kids are asleep
when I hear them: hedgehogs,
fighting over the cat's saucer.

There's no-one around,
not even Mike, who goes mad
on the stairs and has built

a wrestling-ring next door
(it sways gently against my fence,
searching for *lebensraum);*

or Robbie, who took on a gang
of drunks one Saturday while we
watched from the gallery.

They are in hog mode tonight,
screeching, fleet of foot,
Jupiter's moons gone apeshit.

They spin the disc that cheers,
splashing milk islets everywhere
as our angels drift on, open-mouthed.

Roadside Badger at Allt-yr-Fach

You could make something of this –
the body in the gutter,
its blood race forming sunset deltas;
bellowed songs of vengeance;
bad Samaritans on the cusp of a stench.

Then there's the cold eye,
assessing the value to *Melis melis*
of this dissenter's quaint odyssey –
abraded incisor, missing claw;
and the gut contents: small bleached
mammals, a pebble, impregnable seeds.

But it's enough as it is:
the twisted balls sticky as tar;
flies jewelling a broken snout
(Mr Midnight's come-uppance);
and the others back there,
nudging a moonlit absence.

Fireflies

Cruising to 'a land of romance',
our feet grey with scuffed embers,
we knew it was not an act of recovery
spurred by advertisements of young love –
but one of fumbling remembrance.
Snapshots fractured by fear and the cold,
my want of courage, your dimmed horizon
as we waited, muffled, for the 'result'.
In those days, I guess, kept close by a pair
of midwife toads, silently spawning
in a place where the talk was
of other outcomes (points scored, success,
and the late pleasures of chant and ale).

We fought, of course, even there,
in the world of the doleful male,
as you called it, and women made fibrous
by load-bearing of one sort or another.

Then, banished at night till we dropped
from our separate heights, unmoved again,
I saw them in the field below, their neon tracks
stitching, stitching, blindly mending.

Killed on the Ice

is a verdict we were always being given
to explain the fates of the missing.
We saw them mock-courageous among the floes, playing
their games of catch-as-catch-can
until black lightning flailed them backwards,
their cries for help mimed in the distance.

But we knew their timidity, their trepidation,
how they would call us to the waterfront
and, barred by the wonders of rigor –
its machinations in the depths, its congealing power –
point to the first thrusting crystals on the ebb
then, upstream at an angle, the blocked trajectories.

Fading

Mrs M is now defined by things not done:
the phone left unanswered; a slipped roof tile
stalled by oozing moss. Last in the competition,
her sunflowers are over, those bad losers
conferring in their arena of rust.

Her only child spoke once: 'You can't stay here.'
But his words were lost in the drift of down,
the airborne Allied landings. A faraway don, he warns
of the Pathetic Fallacy as her specs in the sun
semaphore to neighbours without reply.

She rang the doorbell once a year
to update herself on twelve-month-old gossip.
Bright as a button, we said, hoping remembrance
would not tip to a halt, to a moraine,
with a view of day blotting up night.

If only she knew this is her element:
the ice cataracts;
the fox in the outhouse;
the eczema of paint peeling.

Time was When

caterpillars showed off
    in fur coats
        or attended mass meetings
            of the Wasp Impersonation Society

cuckoo babies turned dolls out of cots
    and stole your mother,
        while fathers went out straight
            and came back crooked, learning to speak

kingfishers and dragonflies
    could never stay long;
        sticklebacks mouthed protests in jars;
            toadspawn turned to music

dirty old men were
    A-certificate guides to films
        which sometimes pegged out early
            among noisy, searchlit mourners

birds laid enough eggs to pinprick,
    their blown innards oozing,
        like a rubberman escape artist
            forbidden to thrash a way out

parents left odd things in drawers:
    inner tubes for a giant's burnt finger;
        bathing hats for midgets;
            grease they ate for 'movement'

hawthorns sprouted bread and cheese
  and potatoes had babies underground;
    Mr Morley approached a door death owned,
      after trimming his high laurel

ice closed down canals;
  fathers drove kids to the seaside
    to turn pink and be peeled;
      living-room fires wouldn't share heat

granny died like your hamster
  but no-one dug a hole under the apple-tree;
    instead they took her away, arms behind backs,
      then filled their own cheeks with sandwiches

Severn Bore

i.m. Ivor Gurney

Newnham is where we wait for it;
below Minsterworth, your orchard home.

The undertowing tide has stolen away
with the corruption of the night.

On the far bank, a bird pipes
in the clean-sheet morning.

Two otters slalom through the reeds,
but that covenant is broken:

no need now to escape the flood –
the gulls are decoys plunged in silt.

Nomad surfers, the votaries of Bayreuth,
pull on their skin to meet a punctual god.

Then it is spotted beyond the ox-bow
by voiceless outriders waving flags.

Thunder? said the sexton to the little boy –
why, that's Mick bowling marbles;

and this, too, combing the sleek islets,
rolls in with its baggage, its flailing victims:

we rush to Minsterworth (where reason slept),
along the road crawled by murderers.

The Housatonic at Stockbridge

I warned her there was nothing
behind the silences, no running waters,
deep or otherwise, and I wondered
what she saw in me. I did have
a nice line in terse and vivid description:
that dark horse stuff, for instance,
I told her was like rushing to a tap,
turning it on and having nothing happen.

She probably said she'd twist my faucet
any time, sunshine; and she did,
ever ready before due order of precedence –
no shoving the canoe down the bank
but swimming out to deep midstream, where
it was already sleek and stiff in her grip,
her imagining. It was an American thing,
apparently, as they all had their shrinks.

Mention of water reminds me of her hair;
it was the rust-red of peat juice sluicing
down the lee of Ingleborough to Pecca Falls –
so many fiery seams in the polished drop to froth –
and it had its irksome, inbuilt cascades,
the sort of thing you could do nothing with
on bad days; and there'd be plenty, the plopping
of fizzy tablets in my glass notwithstanding.

We really didn't know what I wanted,
which was a charitable way of putting it,
very Stateside, though there were enticements,
aqueous things in the wild: the great falling Potomac;
lakes viewed Pizarro-style from the Adirondacks;
Walden Pond, which she'd zoomed on to
like an astronaut aiming to land in a puddle;
and another place, some river in Massachusetts

she said couldn't be seen moving downstream,
so much like ice was its midge-mad surface.
And I think of that sly current when recalling
the evening we died below Farleton Fell –
broken down and under tow, I guided our wreck
while she sat with the Samaritan in his car,
her tresses in spate as she gasped and laughed,
some go-anywhere pick-up on Route 66.

Recorded Poet

College guys in a fish tank
signal Go (the shellac's spinning)
and he scans the flea-jump phrases
in that hickster-voiced
guide to complexity,
which says: This is new;
this is looking from above.
His right foot stomps,
a bird flutters in his chest.

But they couldn't delete
the plane landing, a car revving,
the overhead train.
(Mitzi is flying home to her folks;
Nussbaum needs a new clutch;
Mrs Pallola ducks a switchblade
between Pelham and Bronx Park East.)

Oh, how he sings for them down the years
on all their mad night journeys!

Draughtsman

A missive from the Front
was how Fran described it –
her Johnny's note, as though he'd nudged
a beetle through an ink blob.
Under each line – a sketch
really, a prospect of hills –
her translations were words
set to strange music. *Winterreise*,
journey towards madness and death.
Far back, he'd made his own wedding-suit:
Fran's mother tut-tutting
to the crunch of his scissors
through bolts of prickly serge
and leant on top secrets
at a sunlit de Havilland window.
The simpering smile was well-meant:
worlds of wanting turned on it
until his headaches storm-clouded
and he drew the tumour for us,
'No bigger than a golf ball' –
plan, elevation, floating segment.

We got there in April, our concern
so much gilt on the care of others.
It made a faint flash, like his anger,
as he contemplated a pear-tree,
Fran's petalled bathing-cap
on his tufted, balding head
hiding 'the business, the Big T'.

Tsunami

We never knew where you were,
Sumatra; now, your irruption
Has moled into the lawn, destroying
Our nice view: yellow jasmine,
Fields of promising winter wheat,
The lane searched by sunsets.

Sumatra – you reminded us of
Anahorish in your lightness of consonant;
Your ironed-out syllables
Flattened everything to silence;
We gaped at your good fortune,
Tongued your sweet food from trees.

But, Sumatra, you carried a portent:
Your land is a beached raft of the medusa,
Though 'Su' is the lightest of zephyrs
And 'matra' a double benediction.

Teach us your old lesson, Sumatra –
Something soothing, some mantra.

Miners at the Quarry Pool

Though one were strong as seven, He too with death shall dwell...

Algernon Charles Swinburne, *The Garden of Proserpine*

Here where the whirr is quiet,
bodies scrubbed pink
lollop in black water, black

as the seam they pick
between granite shunting
at Springvale face.

All shapes, all ages disport,
their sullen Arcadia free
of the hymn's earshot.

Water washes: sleepy wives
penetrated, whippets starved in sheds,
benefactors wished into dying –

each act purified with the boys'
night guilt in these icy,
mollifying depths.

Davies, pear-shaped survivor
of Six Bells and Senghenydd,
pinches his nose like an old fop

and bombs the luckless Watkins,
who cried mute inglorious
when a pony slumped in the shafts,

pinning him three miles below
with flicked images
of the unremembered dead.

Elsewhere they strut and pose,
arms folded, their dicks
in motion like the stirring chrysalis.

Morgan slides down a rainbow
while Grenville the walrus
surfaces, incisors glowing.

Cadwallader is a smudged ghost,
Owens a trussed torso, the others a menace
of loins gathering, flecked with scars.

A steam-whistle shrieks
and there go the loves that wither,
the old loves with wearier wings.

Kindertoten

Tabernacle Chapel, Ty'n-y-Pant

Safe in the bosom of Jesus
they all lie counted in a walled fold
beneath abandoned Ty-Mawr,
farmhouse of the everlasting penance,
which is giving birth to another stone.

Survivors in their wrath have dumped
old tractors across the fell,
flayed horses and starved sheep,
because they made it to fifty,
toiling below the innumerable stars.

Berg's violin concerto commemorates
an 'angel' – it soars at the end
after much thunder, as sunlight
rallies this plot, climbing the wall
like a little juice-smudged scrumper.

Two American Photographs

Margaret – were you grieving for those specks unleaving;
and did you want to say when you banked left to pray
that, without deceiving, the scene you snapped that day
was what gods, believing, see when they turn away?

To that couple, perhaps, the bride in windy wraps,
the guests below with necks so cricked that sex
has vanished from the maps that burly best-man Tex
and friends in well-meant lapse have plotted with her 'ex'.

And what of young Mary: quite to the contrary
grown up to marry Frank, bestower of some rank;
or (and this is scary) by dint of divine prank,
her luck secondary, is strangled by some crank?

Decisive moments tell us nothing so we dwell
on what was or might be away from cloud and sea:
how Marshall later fell (Yolanda's first decree),
and Mary, though a belle, from shoreline deaths must flee.

Climate Change

We moved to a place where the blackcap
was overwintering, much to our relief,
because in its small way it presaged
snowless seasons and falling green ice
(though not all had changed: the female
is red-hooded but remains subsumed),
and the idea that ours might be two
among many deaths, including seas and canyons.

Then, one November, cold killed a lot.
It was forecast but not explained.
Hardy plants were deflowered, frost
infiltrated platoons of winter wheat.
We agreed our fallacies were pathetic,
but there was no mistaking the revenge
of an implacable force, laying, velvet-gloved,
the executioner bird on the window-sill.

Serenade

She's seen it all before,
so puts on a sleepy show
of obedience and allows
this polished Seville *cuadrado*
to take the weight
of the carter's orange load.
He poses, oblivious to urchins
who sneak the fruit, cataracting
his pyramid of plenty.

*

On the Smyrna pier,
big Spiros breaks the legs
of the burden-carriers.
They, too, are unimpressed,
flicking their lashes at fate
and milling to a point.
He's into his rhythm:
two swipes and they buckle
headlong into the sea.

*

Now, in Al Fallujah,
one stands, foot rucked,
flayed by rocket tails.
She's delivered the launcher
for her ignorant victims,
but a soldier's rifle
cannot deflect her
from the grounded enigma
forever three steps ahead.

Trapped Moles Hanging from a Fence at Penrhos Farm

are a tear-out of a Scarlatti sonata,
   or her old man's multitude of socks left
out to dry beyond the point of caring;
   or heads spiked atop a traitors' gate,
that resistance on downward impact
   the bite of raw ox-liver on prodding fork.
She could play; she lived History;
   but dates just waltz in her head with the tunes
and she'd never defy the placard in the hedge
   or think about that upright in the *Advertiser* –
fifty pounds, needs tuning, buyer collects –
   as prelude to music's return, like the prodigal hand.
Or a warning to outsiders and their polemic:
   these be vermin; this be April's count;
hear the silence of the squealing talpa, see 'im smile;
   and to insiders, signalling wretchedness by washing-line,
wishing Aaron's Field would make him smaller still,
   still smaller as he strolls unseeing between the pelts.

Parade of the Warhorses

Here they come, the scarred survivors,
snorting defiance through flared nostrils
but held to a plod by pike, carronade
and the random engraving of bayonets.
Note the unplated breast – baby's bum
of a rippled codger – now cold to the breeze.

Do you remember them – white zephyrs of Samothrace,
skewed defenders of Adairsville – facing rant and howl,
the hiss of the sabre, the scatter of hot shrapnel?

Make room for the mare that flew over the guns,
the roan flayed in the shafts by the bombardier!
See them glint around dun badges on route to the meadow!

Great Western

My grandmother took care to book
her seat on the London train
so that she faced the engine,
not wishing to be dragged
to the dead end of Paddington.

Temperament buffed by time
allows me to see her below
a bleached shot of Clevedon
in terms of a coarser imagery
than her five-feet-two stood for:

the window strap a horse's dangler,
that rubber flaked out under the seat,
the Kleeneze man next to the corridor,
tent-erecting in his trousers
from Severn Tunnel to Ladbroke Grove.

I don't know, though;
perhaps she saw it all too,
but kept it ranked, her handkerchief
a viper's head dabbing
for grit in a strange boy's eye.

We often mis-read the old,
took them for cloned emissaries
sent down the years by Osborne House
to leather-belt the ungodly
and lock them in whimpering rooms.

With her felt hat and ginger rinse,
she knew where she was going:
to Reading, Taplow, Maidenhead,
Royal Oak, the gentle buffers
of a world pictured in letters home –

and her two daughters, fixed
to the platform, misting towards her
from deepest Edgware and Faversham
through the flowing crowd's exhaling sighs,
past the wheeltapper bowed to his calling.

Resurrection

After Stanley Spencer

The sugar-cube of Capel Bethany
Is as a puritan, pitched sentinel
Beyond the tipsy headstones,
Their weathered words slurred or,
In the case of George Wilson, Rechabite,
Blind in a runnel, green as bile.

Meekly refuting this libel,
And to the clunk of white crucifixes,
They would arise one by one:

The three daughters of Bridget Hope;
The one-eyed farrier Ernest Jones;
The Reverend H. H. Leonard (needing a hand);
The infant Mary Winston,
Leeched to the breast of Elsie Winston;
And a surveying regiment of Gwythers,
Their mausoleum a house of cards.

Newscasts

The day Kennedy was shot
I was thieving from the reference library:
Diem's *Uber Die Melancholie,* because
of my grandfather, then three days
silent under the apple tree.

Comrade Temerova was meteoring
by the time my daughter lay
like a sick plant under a cloche.
We'd look up at the window,
where a light meant life yet.

I could only see Nixon fibbing,
though the kids had the volume up
ready for *Top of the Pops*:
I was thinking of her thinking of me
thinking there can be no escape – none.

My father died on the night
they invaded the Gulf, that war
fought on screens: obliteration in a puff
beneath the searching crucifix,
the green tracery my old man's revival.

Now, I've found a lump (as they say),
just when experts were explaining acid rain:
all that pond life fanning towards
its sizzled death unseen, then spiralling
down in the dark, out of it.

Reel Time

The Great Warriors are taking it easier:
slower is the advance on Vimy Ridge.
No need to dash, as in the excitable days:
the sprint's a squelching trot across No Man's Land.

But let's not rush to join in the decelerations
of that over-wound clockwork march on Antwerp,
the speedy Miracle of the Marne.
Blink and you'd missed them –
and those Frenchies biding no time at all.
Was that an exhortation to hold Verdun?
Run it by me again. And those Ottomans,
twitching as if swarmed by the common flea,
its life-history a twinkle at the old rates.
Washing on the Siegfried Line used to dry in a trice,
victory crowds smoke a fag in three seconds.

Now it'll never be over by Christmas.
Enlisters stop rehearsals for the walking race;
a painter slowly brushstrokes Ferdy's assassination;
but at least those lights going out across Europe
will allow us to get used to the dark.

Dilemma

Johnny Williams is on his speedy,
Saturday-night march past our house,
a gallon of Hancock's on board
yet only one step in five off course;
and him haranguing all the while
the aproned missus who's reeling him in.
Stand here and watch this, my grandfather said
on the August evening I first saw Johnny walk
as if he were a one-man parade
illustrating a slightly crooked mile of sin.

Five years on and the distance would impress –
the time it took to make a moral point
about a sinner whose double waywardness
seemed less notable than his indestructibility,
which for a grandparent wondering
what was going on in his nether parts
after a signed pledge long unbroken
required a return from me of a resolute gaze
that searched for what I'd actually go for:
pleasure or the questionable benefits of sobriety.

Helmand

I've come down to the cellar now,
    where the sounds of all those birds
hurling themselves at my window
    are so many faraway thuds topside.

They've all tried it over the years.
    That surviving woodpecker was a hoot,
winking and on its back in the border,
    feet curled to kestrel's talons.

Mustn't forget the kamikaze tits –
    or the thicko thrushes and blackbirds,
lone Wellingtons scudding across the lawn
    forty feet above the Wadden with me

Scotty, Jigger and Chalky no longer
    encapsulated but up front as light as air
after flash-frying a thousand Germans;
    then 'Home James!' through pledged moonlight.

God, the boy's gone – man down – in Marjah.
    Twenty-one. When he was just six
I remember him cupping that yunker starling,
    a berry of black blood pincered in its beak.

Everything dead then had gone to heaven,
    so we buried it; and on that night of vigil
it rose through a headlight's sweep,
    the slow upward fluttering of a soul.

I didn't tell him, because kids forget;
    nor did I mention that roadkill badger at Henllys
or the blackcap neatly prostrate at our new place.
    His message was delivered, sure as a swift.

Approaching Maes-y-Gwenith

My father's slow white Vauxhall,
rolling towards me in a dream
through sluiced fieldwaters,
is Pegasus, Bellerophon
attacking the Solymi and Chimaera.
Keats's symbol of poetic vision.

But these were just imaginings
bequeathed to us grammar boys
while he tramped the streets
for weekly debtors, a mortal
raised from the Cambrian's inspection pit
and its clinging isomorphs of grease.

Though water still layers the road,
buzzing atoms of his car
huddle now in Paulo's cooking range
and Monsieur Faucheux's gleaming bike
while, shimmering, he watches,
starred by Zeus above Gray Hill.

Incident at The Cayo

You could be mad in those days:
A Manny Bumford, eyeing the brolly
On a woman's lap at the doctor's
Then snapping it clean across his knee;
Or an Aubrey Harvey, that puffing troll
Astride the gully in Church Road.
Barmy shufflers bouncing
From road to pavement – you crossed over
When their front doors loomed
Or met them face to face, their eyes
Spinning at some crazy event in your hair.
Only the grown-ups were fearless,
Pitying them as stunted coevals.

But you, too, come at last
To the empty threat of witlessness:

Sold-up Iolo Bevan keeps an ewe alive,
Grateful for the time she's taken,
The shaven fleece, her providence
At each of his whistled-in years.
They say he's done with killing;
The pit dug for that whiskered nag
He hauled to the lee of Gray Hill
Saw him slip away by degrees.
He'll wheel the sheep out in time,
To meet his senses in the wild rye.

War Memorial Hospital

We are the lads who muck out
The crackling lungs of the vets.
Rain pricks our porters' hut
Like stray arrows of Agincourt;
Chalky's element this; war's his thing:
Books with planes in bird silhouette,
Cutaway tanks and stripped Kalashnikovs.
He hates my conshie lunchtime reading:
just now *Guillain-Barre Syndrome –*
Early Descriptions of Ascending Paralysis.
He can spy Guillain at Salpetriere
Next to the aproned dissector, posing
Like Proust and a Metropol chef
Before the neat carving of livers.
The blokes in Six are death-feigned;
We have helped pound their chests
And milked our daily spittoon's-worth
Caused by the Kaiser's wafted mustard gas.
Chalky's penknife nicks another victory
While I, abstracted, feel myself
Blotting you through tissue and membrane.
Last night, your fingers stopped speech soft
On my lips and traced Achilles' tendon,
Contaminating me with the promise
Of your wild, foreign love
(*toe, foot, thigh, glutei, adductor*).
Chalky says he eats pussy and fancies hole
After pummelling his 'dead meat'.
(*The intellectual faculties are preserved*

Until the end; the danger of asphyxiation
Is always imminent; death is avoided by
Downward remission of the illness.)
Will you, too, slip from my body,
Hands palming your suffused remnant
Over contracture, delirium, convulsion,
Leaving me spittle-chinned, a pale casualty
Staring up heroic towards the light?

A Juror at the Tea Dance

That lunchtime I was slow getting away
from the courtroom, where one could be so sure
of matching a man with his hovering fate
and, if pushed, might be disinclined to say
he did it because he was sick or poor
or had justification for his hate.

No doubt I would on any other day
have sauntered idly through the market door
to pass the time or now, at any rate,
give vent to a sixty-year-old's dismay
at how a lovely building's lost its core,
the restoration ugly and too late.

I went upstairs, and at one end a ray
of light – no-one could really want for more –
was passing through stained glass that had to wait
on a craftsman's pleasure but, anyway,
was finished as the new laminate floor
bowed beneath much ceremonial freight.

Drinking coffee at Maisie's Bar I may
in that brief rainbow beam have sensed a pure
form of joy that, lacking a present mate,
my status as one who had lost his way,
perhaps, explained a movement or a lure
among a group of widows to my right.

By any stretch she looked a little fey,
my would-be partner, obeying the law
that says – My dear, one should not under-rate
a lone and likely male's need to inveigh
against neglect, ruination and flaw
and ask the judge of all to hesitate.

Kelston Horse-trough

Time has blurred the date
as Mr Stiles has lost
sight of reflection,
his means of damming the years
that now spill everywhere.

The spout's an elephant
head in pewter, trunk chipped,
obliterate free spirit
of Empire, its culvert
a trickle from Lansdowne heights
as though the Ganges
had come to this; or as
if the snow-melts had begun.

The lifeless crock is now art:
a picture by Matisse,
cool glaze and earthy depth,
phthalo and mantis green
gown sliming to the dark;
and – late replacements
for the past and passing snouts –
stiff digits of goldfish.

Time's a Wiesler here,
cleric No. 124, stamping
events that don't concern,
leaving just fond remnants,
images of the grand picturesque –
no trudging without water,
no elephantine wars fought for others,
no surfing the map's flood tide.

Revenants

The old may be living longer and therefore growing in number; but their chief characteristic is that for many, particularly the young, they remain invisible.

US magazine report

That girl at the till, for instance.
Her mind elsewhere as I complained
about a dud battery and made some point
about the decline in the quality of things;
she replaced the item and just stared through me without
so much as a Yes, No, Oh or Thanks.
Ever present, with her mind on the future
(another boy to meet, the smart one
at Dylan's the previous Saturday perhaps),
she regards me as someone out of bounds,
another ambling tenant of the past
come grasping to the fence for alms.

So, among the phantoms, I play a game,
imagine my transparency to be an advantage –
you know, seeing the unseeing as haunted
and in their blindness, their unconcern,
the innocence that might stir my pity
and my spectre's frustration that a bit later
in a queue herself and her mind on the future
(a woman to meet, the one at the clinic
the previous week perhaps; or a report
to pick up from the consultant),
she recalls the sweet Dylan's boy – dead

in the highway – and the one who replaced him,
out with the lads that night and home late,
swaying in the dark at the foot of the bed, undermining
the sleep she's learned to feign.

Salva Fleschmann at Eighty

A marquee
    goes up
in that garden
    where silver
trees form a
    Birkenwald
in which each
    year a swarm
of bluebells,
    as soon gone
as come
    for something none
can give bar
    prognosis
(but bluebells
    just the same),
crowds to
    the striped lawn's edge,
gatecrashers,
    if she's timed
it right,
    as she's wont to.

There's a Break in the Tree-line

was all my father said,
except for some stuff
about his leaking pond, car troubles
and the usual trash on TV.

It's there when I drive over
to occupy my mother's space
in that home without its maker,
where brittle crumbs drift in crevices,
wet spoons crust the sugar
and the penalty of things not done
advances towards the widower's redoubt
like a platoon on its stomach –
or the trees themselves, cresting
the ridge of Mynydd Maen
before we were born, but petrified now
by the endless patience of foresters.

It had long gained its height,
the bleached roots lusting deep
for the mountain's quicksilver streams;
the years had refined it,
winds combed out its excess,
honed all to sharp intolerance
as Monty collected his freedom,
Uncle Joe wiped legions off the map,
and chimps meteored among the stars –
each to be stifled by a call
across whose wavering words

fell the shadow of thugs
come for their confession.

I saw them – a gap left
by the advancing forester,
the flash of the swung axe.

Reserved Occupation

You never went to war, *mein Vater,*
Caught you packet deep
In that grease monkeys' temple,
Grimacing by lamplight under
Trucks revving for battle:
The platoons queuing for those anthems
Of yours stretched on the rack.

Where was it they sent you?
Some Craiglockhart for non-combs,
Exponents of the twenty-hour day,
Plodders frozen by the mystery
Of no longer wanting to cope?

And your collier father before,
Hacking out a deeper burrow
Than all his mates had at Havrincourt,
Tame, pick-triggered sparks
Mimicking the icy starburst
They wrote home to Sis about
In the fingerless mittens she'd made.
He found stillwater silence, too;
Lived on, their keen progenitor,
To learn of Watson and Crick,
Fates spiralled in helices.

And here I am now, waiting
For news from another front
Beside this bed in this monument
To bright dew and bloody sweat.
(Is that why we fought two wars?
Friends asked, watching a TV suit
Slither between title and privilege.)
Surgeons stitch another's chest sans lung –
Defences held for another day –
But they'll soon be back at base
To say your wounds are fatal.
You knew all along, of course.

I see only your pillowed head,
Guess at the tucked-in rest of you,
Proliferating madly beyond the end,
And I wonder if the dark's for me,
Whose life is mere skirmishing,
Will choose me for the Fallen
Who has lived to mourn the numberless
And, with time others bought,
Watched, waiting, the housemartins –
Hirundines – wheeling in again,
Mercury fled from Mars,
The cycle advanced.

Catchphrase

There were no striding celebs then,
Just voices in the molten wireless
As we horse-shoed around the grate,
Gods in the gods, to watch
The mice enter upstage right
Then vanish at the twitch of a nose
Or a sudden, drumming finger.

'Get in there, Moreton!' was one,
From Horne, Murdoch or Askey,
Each working a studio audience
And its knots of mirth
Like Lloyd's boy whistling sheep –
Moreton the fall guy,
Who only ever wanted out.

We'd hitched ourselves to Lammer Price,
The same Lammer bound to die
Steep on the water-chute at Porthcawl –
A pennant-flapping balsa thicket –
And we snuggled in the Welfare bank
To watch them build the ring
When Driscoll's Booth came.

They seemed a mile away at least
In that long night of hunkering,
Of sucking the bitter grass stems:
Moreton the pale light-heavy
Poking at tumble-haired Killer O'Doyle.
'Get in there Moreton!' Lammer shouted
To the sound of laughter in the wind.

Removing your Hat for a Funeral

They used to do it all the time:
old men who'd taken an hour to dress;
drunks leaving the Feathers in mid-lurch;
a Down's boy after a practical demo.

Even the bare-headed at least stopped,
no matter who was creeping off the coil
or how many darkened the trailing wake:
all those doleful heads on coins.

Death is now too much without us:
the old soldiers, the toddling babes,
their medalled mourners in berets
and their sugar-mouse coffins.

With lusty kissing in public,
standing and doffing must have
survived somewhere, some place
of side-by-side civilities.

Imagine streets of respectful folk;
frozen multitudes nodding;
sad avenues of lovers entwined;
titfers tipped in pastures of love and death.

Elegies

To your grandson in the apple-tree
you must have been fore-shortened,
already telescoping, V-shaped, to a point;
yet it was you who saw Ariel,
a wand rippling the blossom
with its lethal fishtail of spray.
Who would have thought it –
a careless image, unsurprising,
for which your giddier son
alone must always perform
a balancing-act with mere words.

*

I knew they would break on the descant: tears,
for the counter-tune that tows bright melody
into the province of shadow. These walls once bent
to your marriage vows but stiffen now to the swell
of singers on the wing, who will crave your alto,
a subtler voice as unsung as your ministering
to the ancient and lame, beyond festive chanting.

*

Death Notice gives way to Thanks for Sympathy
on my laden screen, line by line deleted,
like trains rushing night legions to oblivion.

*

We'd gone out to take the mind off things
as though our grief could be dumped and forgotten,
but I saw the sky steel-blue above Allt-Fach
and Sirius etched above that lulling point
where the slope begins its headlong fall;

and a figure, some night-rambler, come to the ridge
by degrees to ponder a while then depart,
until there was nothing but the other stars,
livid, too, in their consortia.

Semper ad Meliora

We first saw them innocent from the new-
intake balcony. Through the sea of boys
parted by 'Moses' Morgan, they tripped like
characters out of an old book, she
in front, bowed, her hobble skirt sweeping the floor
and 'Prof' behind, wearing shades as dark
as obsidian, his egghead uplifted
by winged collar and tight cravat, one arm,
a measurement, outstretched to her sprouting
nape. Older and downstairs with the breaking
wavelets, we saw them close up – his sweat, swabbed
cuts and shuffling pumps; her bag of knitting
and plug of Polos, their old decorum.
They sat to play for hymns, the page-turning
days a prequel. (It was the last Woodbine
before the drop, the night of love
before embarkation, an ecstasy
among Christian soldiers.) For 5C's sappers
were at work elsewhere with tape and tripwire
on his Bechstein, a patient under
the stealthy knife, waiting to be Trojan-horsed
into position, the boys' giggling
a *decrescendo*. His first two-fisted chord
would do it, an opening offensive
of clatter as the innards scudded
their soft shrapnel, mimicking the Wrigley-size
tab that defiled his temple on the Marne.

After detention once, I heard him play
Chopin alone and embraced the door,
with my face twisted against the glass, lips
a pair of mating slugs. Guilt was tunnelling
beneath the mischief lodged in my bone
like the whizzing fragment that first put out
his light, when she appeared behind, her mint
and camphor the outriders, and gently
touched me. I looked along her trembling,
engageant sleeve, a measurement, outstretched
to my aching neck. Mazurka slipped
to nocturne (starlight, the guns mute, save for
a bright falling flare), which accompanied her
benediction, plea for release, healing
touch – acts a spudhead dullard, pen down, would
(surly, depraved) ever leave unremarked.

Nuptials

A photo came to me
of my parents' wedding,
a wartime union notable
for the Degas composition
of a snapper trying to be formal
with a tripod, and sending
an image down the years
of my father and mother
with a random uncle and aunt,
who are gazing at something out of shot
and not noticing my old man's
pained features, as though even
then he was snagged by the guts-ache
that would double him daily
till he died sixty years later
of something unrelated for
which he had no cupboard stash of pills –
his suffering mirror image
opening on to its patent relief –
and I'm thinking that this ready-made
expression was for every time I hurt him,
as though I was bound to let him down,
and that here he is still willing me
to prove that I could go one better
and be what he couldn't, beguiled
by the light that brings
just another day, temperate, save for dreaming.

Glossary

It's deliberately way down
on our list of things to discuss,
though being the bastard it is
the proclamations are up front –
under her silly bobble-hat,
in her late, wren-like reduction,
in the pyrrhic bravery of the sick.

By the time it surfaces
we're discussing chemo,
metastasis, all illness's arcana;
and I'm a fantastic voyager,
being swept along her conduits,
like a correspondent, to observe
cities fallen, risen again or under siege.

But it needs no metaphors
incapable of being shared,
just the syllable-fortified
mesothelioma, immunotoxin,
extravasation and dysphagia
and those devices they echo:
catapelta, strappado, mancuerda.

Axeman

That monster looming out of the night
is next door's pollarded willow. I think
Bert has overdone it this time, but assures
us that it will come again, like the Jewsus Christ
he's always appealing to when, aloft
with that tool he says was made for the job,
his footing gives and he nicks a finger.
Sometimes he's like the Holy Son himself,
his flurry of wounds by jab and prick
dulled as he weaves his way home
from the Crown, dropping to his knees
every ten yards on route to Crossways.

But he'll be risen by six the next morning
and hacking back old growth in an hour,
the night's mattress mould dissolving
as surely as his knobbly creations will again
shake their spears at him, given a winter to re-group.

Tarzan

Me shady, you clean-cut;
you lively, me blank.

You honest, me shifty;
me scaredy, you frank.

Me indoors, you windblown
you pumping, me puffed.

You open, me shutcase;
me cussed, you chuffed.

Me paleface, you ruddy;
you brainy, me dull.

You pretty, me ugly;
me emptied, you full.

Me careless, you thoughtful;
you reading, me read.

You fated, me willing;
me sobbing, you dead.

At the Lautrec Exhibition

She comes daily from a screaming house
To sit beneath Aristide Bruant,
Spotlit for the silent *cognoscenti*,
Who crowd to stare through her.

The curator almost wet himself
Explaining the sentinel power
She would wield over an imported *oeuvre*,
But the tripping smiles mean

She's dozed off again, dreaming
Of her neighbour, Signore Scardovi,
The Mighty Mouse, shushing stragglers
From Santa Maria Matricolare.

A chuckle bullets her body
As the Mouse croons past
Titian's Assumption like an usherette
Letting the A feature roll again.

Skeleton

You are arched over the runnels
Your fingers had drawn;
In your quilted paradise
Each parcel bleeds its colour;
A Birnam Wood of tomato plants
Gives of its coming fruitfulness,
Like an overture.

You left apples on the bough
For birds to crater in Autumn,
And made slugs writhe in slime
Ready for Spring's old wars,
When azaleas beaconed the path
To your soft-raked beds
And I awarded your silhouette
Papery onions from a tray.

Yet, in Winter you scanned unseeing
A garden of mere outline
Beyond dolorous window panes.
A drawer was open behind us,
Its chessmen Bramleys rotting for once
On farmed-out Daily Mirrors
As if to confound your notions
Of a tender rout of bitterness.

Aristocracy

Each night at eight in our spelican season
the crows convene at Coker's Wood.

Though litter-blown, they form a hierarchy of sorts:
laboured dignity of elders, pitch and dip of bucks.

In this corridor a pair will dogfight exalted buzzards,
deposing them, squawking at their flight into exile.

Painted jays, plummeting like native birds of paradise into
the luscious trees, cannot rise to their occasion.

Sometimes they band, mock the cabaret of tits,
fall in with lout starlings, pick at livers done for them.

But these are forays; they strop, roost, build heavenwards.
They stay high-up, cloaked partygoers.

Fate

Pepito slivers through the letterbox,
skids on the Bright World tiles
to crave a donation at my feet.

A fiver will keep him alive
for a week, it says, or cut
his mother's long trek to the pump.

I'm a Houdini, shackled by guilt:
Who works these things out, anyway?
How come ten quid lifts a cataract?

Pepito beds himself down
between pizza flyer and mortgage advance,
but he can't get to sleep.

Extra sheets arrive by post
to make him more comfortable;
then he's stacked for refusing

to behave. By the weekend
he'll be bruised in the bin,
a flower opening on a dark stench.

Training Camp, 1914

You could tell 'em a mile off:
Cheeseborough the stiff-kneed bull,
waiting for his blindfold
and the ripped cloth across the heart.

Toff Boniface from the Hall
(all glossy in his Sam Brown),
bred for shagged-out lurching
towards the first Hun battery.

Cor Blimey Bill from Hackney,
up and down in the Empire gods –
and on the Meuse as like –
pissed in his helmet, sniper fodder.

and wide-mouthed Private Meryvane,
Lincoln furrows breaking in his eyes,
huddled sheep in Radnor, a Midlands room.
For him a shell to shatter his illusions.

Nightjars

You can guess who first pointed them out.
That's right: motormouth, the big show-off,
the slimy bastard, The Old Dissembler.
We were going home late from his flat
when he braked beside a place called
Oak Park (everything sloping down to water
ringed with trees), some town's benighted core.
We slid off the back seat, his two 'little ones',
and pressed against the railings like him.
All he said was, 'Listen, prisoners, listen.'
First we could hear the hum of the lights
behind us and 'the denizens all abed',
as he describes it in *Drifters at Dusk*.
Then, called into being by the intensity
of putting our minds to it, we heard them:
the nightchurrs churring, perhaps just two,
that drilling unceasing in its hell haven
down there, forbidden by padlock and chain.

She was still up when we got home at two.
There was a tired balestra, lunge and fleche;
but he was soon gone, well out of it.
Upstairs in our heaven haven we remembered
the bad times, the guttural nightsparring
from below, the room screeching with light
as they began irretrievably breaking down.

Organist

He played the harmonium in his front room, pedalling
to the border of some promised land of music,
where lucid seconds of delight hovered for the taking,
like a rainbow – or Battastini, pinned between the babel
of Oslo and Hilversum on his fretworked wireless.

It never came to much. He sat astride
a chapel organ which piped his shortcomings
as hymn singers took their leave. When arthritis folded
his hewer's fingers away, he watched a Wurlitzer starbursting
from Odeon depths, its rhinestoned rider grinning.

Another Arundel Tomb

What will survive of us is love,
especially if the stonemason
was told to portray them that way,
despite the complexity of
their case. Did he take her while
she slept? Did she play the field?
Did the mutts at their feet take
the point of those *sabatons* up
their arse? Who is to say
this conceit of sun-blessed charm
is not a fib, seen by the lanky poet
as time's gift for all his altered folk
but meant to hide the fact that he
was clanking stud and she a slut?

But consider the tomb
of Joan de Vere or Alice FitzAlan – no-
one is sure who lies within –
missed by the bike-clipped bard, perhaps
because her interest is below,
among the mourning figures bent
to her fame, whatever it was;
her blemishes have not been sluiced
to leave some unintended mark,
some blazon that really tells all
we need to know about our kind,
but her anonymous ranking
has long been head-to-toe complete
and those weepers, straining beneath,
shed their tears for chip and gouge,
the silent scratch and bruising of
sweet features and a fighting name.

Lives

Grant's manacled rebel, stiff with self-absorption,
blindfolded on the bridge, soon to be dropped,
prays for a slipshod hangman – and the river,
carrying him away to a frantic wife in Tuscaloosa.

As Pizarro's infantry creep lice-like through the forest to
some jutting peak destined to glorify the pretence
of making a raw world roll beneath his feet,
young men born to sacrifice crouch in sunbeamed huts
on the plains of Petan-Eza, some recalling brothers leaping,
and dappled harts sniffing the wind. Others connect,

like Sumerain, who was kissed by generals for spiking
three German guns, yet trudges alone
to the asylum at Madeleine-Bouvet,
where his father has turned into a crazy Marquis.

And when moonmen bounce in puddles of dust, Pritchard,
his fisherman arms unfurling the school photo,
Searches for himself again and again between
Rupert Small   and   Rupert Small,
twin masters of the very slow shutter speed.

The Memory Seats

West Sussex, 2012

They've upped and gone
to eternity, the old wag said

as I stopped at each one
like a council inspector looking

for damage. Absolutely, I replied,
seating myself in Muriel Smith's

vacated place and staring ahead
at groins, pebbles, sea-grey, sky-grey.

I couldn't gainsay his cliché,
still less deny that the loopers and rollers

in the clouds were flying-club smart-arses
and not Wing-Commander Smith

being downed by two Heinkls before
leaving Muriel to long-waltz the remainder

of her span at East Preston; and to pause
at this spot, her favourite, and others.

Capel Bethany

Watch and be ready, for in an hour when ye think not, the messenger may descend

the Rev H. H. Leonard, November 1842

I thought of you tonight,
Now that I am come to this pass:
Two mites in the grave
And my blessed Rachel sick.
I wondered what you preached
On that bright-beam day
When I burned the lime at Rhiw-Las,
Your beard bent, your hair alight,
The silver furrows between us;
Your words breeze-carried,
Falling like flakes, melting.

Kilns are crooked, ploughs ditched,
Our fields hoarse with sheep.

And you are gone to Pisgah,
Too big for your pony;
I christened her Jezebel –
Her tail swished a rebuke
Till you were a dot on Allt-yr-Fach.

Lynton Sands

This summer I know what's going on.
You run for the ball, laugh with the kids,
But a woman has tunnelled beneath your poise.
I can tell from your old salt's sea gaze
That you want to be elsewhere, wish
To smite the alliance of courage and hurt.

You read but no pages turn.
I pick up your book, *The Great Gatsby*,
Wondering if I might hitch a lift
On sentences that trail your thoughts:
'But his heart was in a constant, turbulent riot;
The most grotesque and fantastic conceits haunted him.'

Words I loathe – tryst, affair – spin like midges;
I feel tethered full-fathom, my hair streaming
While the wavy multitude kiss themselves quick.
At the end I, too, shall withdraw to the swell,
Legs astride the Orca inflatable you bought,
Fighting its intent to squirt from under me.

Coda

I wake up to leaves
on the ground, the bottom line.

They've fallen in the night
with none to witness

their removal and descent,
the silent congregation of masses.

Drunk on their blush and ochre,
we have all slept on it

and dreamed of the same confounding –
a late smoulder of life before death.

The Last Tattoo

There have been difficulties: the conceit of a bushfire;
painful soles, eyelids risky. Cobwebs sorted the elbows.

But now, this island in its sea of troubles. A portrait,
I think, the school photo tweezered, like a rare stamp.

It'll be small and secreted for the moving circle
to find peering, pointing; a game of hidden-and-seek.

Then, no more spaces on the crowded continent;
the needle to be stayed, its hamster-eye of ink wiped.

I'll be Ariel taking the stage in frock coat and livid visage;
or that missing earl, dyed among careless foreigners.

Notes

‘Ars Longa, Vita Brevis’
The American poet Thomas Lynch is a funeral director by profession.

‘Two American Photographs’
The photographs: Mary Eschner’s near-drowning, Coney Island, New York, 1952 (Margaret Bourke-White); Yolanda and Marshall Jacobs, after being married atop a flagpole, Cosholton, Ohio, 1946 (Allan Grant).

'Glossary'
Catapelta, *strappado* and *mancuerda*. Torture machines of the Spanish Inquisition.

Acknowledgements

Thanks are due to the editors of the following magazines, in which most of these poems first appeared: *Poetry Wales, New Welsh Review, Agenda, Planet, Oxford Poetry, The Seventh Quarry, Outposts, Dreamcatcher, Poetry Salzburg Review, 10th Muse, Envoi, The New Writer, Staple, Poetry Nottingham International, Borderlines, The Interpreter's House, Sarasvati, Poetry and Audience, The Rue Bella, Roundyhouse, Iota, Dial 174, First Time* and *Smith's Knoll.*

Semper ad Meliora and *Salva Fleschmann at Eighty* were submitted at the invitation of the Poetry Salzburg Press for inclusion in *Poetic Pilgrimages*, published in 2011 to celebrate the 80th birthday of James Hogg, the distinguished publisher and champion of British poetry and a former teacher at the University of Salzburg.

Kindertoten was chosen as the featured poem on the website *Poetry Daily* in the Autumn of 2005. *Revenants* was a finalist in the Torbay Poetry Prize 2011.

It can't be easy for one poet to dissect another's work with a view to possibly re-arranging it, so I'm grateful to my editor, Alan Kellermann, for his keen eye, inspired suggestions and wise counsel. If anything here remains unclear or less than effective, it's because my obstinacy prevailed over his diplomacy.

Lightning Source UK Ltd.
Milton Keynes UK
UKOW04f0725271013

219864UK00002B/10/P

9 781909 844063